Computers and Primary Mathematics

INSET materials for the primary school

Jon Kurta

British Library Cataloguing-in-Publication Data.
A catalogue record for this book is available from the British Library.

ISBN 18 74099 70 7
Photographs by Sally Greenhill
Cover illustration by Sue Hillwood-Harris
Typeset by Bookcraft, Stroud
Printed by GPS Printworks Ltd

CONTENTS

Introduction

Historically, the development of IT in schools has been linked to mathematics. Many of the first computers in schools were used by secondary mathematics departments. Activities — often elementary programming using languages such as BBC Basic — were developed by maths teachers in the belief that the logic and reasoning involved would link closely with pupils' mathematical development. By the early 1980s a variety of small structured programs were available for younger children, designed to provide practice in basic skills. These so-called 'drill and practice' programs are still with us today, although often with a modern look to them. The 1980s also saw the development of Logo and turtle geometry in various guises. Here the mathematical learning mode is quite different, with problem-solving and investigation (particularly of shape and space) very much emphasised. Seymour Papert, the inventor of Logo, is considered by many to be a truly visionary educationalist.

As computers have become easier to use, their application has reached almost every curriculum area. Word-processing, desk-top publishing and 'talking books' have transformed aspects of the language curriculum, CD-ROMs bursting with information are available for history and geography, modern technology is integral to music work, and children delight in using computer drawing and painting packages. Increasingly the Internet is used as an educational tool as well.

But what of mathematics? A recent publication by OFSTED, *Reviews of Research in Mathematics Education, 5–16*, concludes that:

> Computers can have a substantial positive impact on pupils' achievement in mathematics.

But which programs to use? With whom? And when? As already stated, 'drill and practice' programs are still with us, and have become particularly popular in the home computing market. Logo and turtle geometry are still advocated by enthusiasts, and are referred to directly in the National Curriculum, but they are used confidently by only a minority of primary teachers. We also have adventure programs, graphical packages, databases and spreadsheets: software that feels mathematical. But, difficulties in using them aside, the learning objectives can often be difficult to discern.

Aims

This book provides an INSET programme lasting from one to three terms, which aims to:

- help teachers use a range of software to enhance their teaching, and children's learning, of mathematics

- provide a comprehensive look at all the different types of program

- suggest useful starting points for activities, and outline their mathematical learning objectives

- look at the issues involved in organising children's effective use of computers

- look at issues involved in integrating children's effective use of computers into various curriculum areas

- help a school become focused on its use of IT and communicate this focus to a wider community

While some schools will want to use the whole INSET programme, others will want to choose activities to suit their needs. This is quite possible, as each activity stands alone and its purpose is clearly indicated.

How this book is organised

Section 1 involves staff in:

- an audit of software

- discussion about the purposes of different packages, linking the uses of these to appropriate National Curriculum statements

- beginning to consider how different software can enhance the learning of mathematics

Section 2 offers starting points for the use of different mathematical software, including activities for staff to try out together and activities to try with children.

Section 3 considers school and classroom issues involved in using computers for mathematics — and looks at the wider implications of computer use.

The appendices include a discussion of the use of the Internet with some useful Web addresses and an annotated list of software publishers.

Software references

Although this book mentions some specific programs, these are usually by way of example only. It is likely that any school will have a wide range of software resources and, indeed, Section 1 includes an audit of these. Computers bought recently are likely to have come bundled with a range of useful software — 'works' programs that include spreadsheet and database modules and drawing programs are common. Nimbus have included a version of Logo with all their 'Window Box' computers, and other educational suppliers include various adventure games and mathematics games.

This book does not provide information about particular software packages, so when an INSET session focuses on a type of software, such as databases, it would be a good idea for the INSET leader to spend half an hour beforehand looking at the particular program the staff will be using. Specifically, it is a good idea to:

- think about, and so pre-empt, possible questions about how it works

- familiarise yourself with the program manual

- think about preparing a sheet of 'Helpful hints when using . . . [name of program]' to complement the more general handouts in this book

Notes to the INSET organiser

If possible, have a computer set up in the staff room for the duration of the INSET programme. Encourage staff to use this, to share ideas and to check on particular aspects of the software.

When doing INSET sessions on IT, it is important to distinguish between:

- workshop sessions designed to increase personal computer skills and confidence (for example, learning the basics of using a spreadsheet), and

- time spent looking at how to use the software with children

During workshop sessions ask the staff to think about adapting the activity they are looking at for use throughout the KS1/KS2 age range. Encourage them to share their experiences in using the software.

Where staff are being encouraged to try activities out with children, you should build time into sessions to review children's work and look at issues about particular software.

During discussion it is important to make time for everyone to voice their concerns. Those who are less experienced in either personal or classroom use of IT may need encouragement to talk, as they may fear seeming more 'backward' than their colleagues.

When tackling issues such as classroom organisation and assessment it is important that the staff move forward as a team. Reaching a consensus can take time, and you should allow for this.

Many teachers lack confidence in both teaching mathematics and using IT, so be wary of using too much jargon or of being the 'technical whiz'. A good up-to-date computer dictionary is a useful purchase for the staffroom. You can also photocopy the vocabulary sheet on page 5, and supply all teachers with a copy.

Planning your programme

Before you begin the INSET programme, assess the needs of the staff. On page 6 there is a questionnaire. Ask staff to fill it in and return it to you before the holidays so that you have some information on which to base your plans for the INSET.

Term 1	Term 2	Term 3
Activity 1 Activity 2 Activity 3 Activity 4 one from activities 5–9 one from activities 11–16	three or four activities chosen from Section 2 and Section 3	three or four activities chosen from Section 2 and Section 3

A whole year's programme of INSET

As the INSET leader you might need to pay particular attention to any 'reluctant computer users' amongst the staff. Talk to colleagues individually about

their concerns outside the staff meetings. Use these occasions to make suggestions for small changes in practice — for example, turning on the computer first thing in the morning, pinning up notes about using a program, using confident children from another class to help younger children with loading and saving work. Make sure you give less confident colleagues attention during the INSET workshops.

In assessing the needs of the staff you could try to take advantage of computer expertise some people may have developed outside school. For example, when you are dealing with spreadsheets, databases and desk-top publishing programs, some members of staff may have software skills that can be shared.

If you plan a one-term programme of INSET, make time to help staff work through some general issues and become clearer about the purposes of using IT for mathematics. If you are short of time, concentrate on just one computer program, rather than many. Developing confidence and expertise throughout the school in one software package is far better than superficially looking at lots of different ones.

If you can continue the INSET program for a further one or two terms you will have the opportunity to look at further software packages and further general issues.

Alternatively you may wish to combine a selection of three activities (one from each section) for a whole or half day's INSET.

Location of INSET

For Activities 1, 4–8 and 10 access to computers is essential, so the location of the sessions needs careful planning. In each case, three adults per computer should be the maximum, although two is better. Is there a hall or classroom into which it is convenient to move a number of computers? If not, it might be necessary to ask staff to disperse to different locations for the 'hands-on' parts of the session. If you must do this, be strict about when you want everyone to return for the final discussion and spend your time circulating amongst the staff, noting any issues that arise for discussion later.

Activity 9 uses floor robots. If you have no more than two of these, try to borrow extra ones from a neighbouring school (offer to reciprocate at a later date) or the local teachers' centre.

Computer vocabulary

Application
a software program for a particular purpose, such as a spreadsheet or a database.

CD-ROM
a popular way to store large multimedia applications and software distribution.

Database
an electronic filing system, useful for organising large amounts of data. Examples include Junior Pinpoint and Information Workshop.

Desk-top publishing
software used to design newsletters and reports. Examples include Microsoft Publisher.

Floor robots (Pip/Roamer)
programmable toys capable of following a series of commands.

Floppy disk
a portable disk, useful for backing up computer work and transferring files between computers.

Hard disk
permanent computer part — stores all essential files and applications.

Hardware
the basic physical components of the computer: base unit, keyboard and monitor.

Interface
a connection between computer parts or between a user and a software application.

Internet
the global network of connected computers. The Web has become the most popular part due to its friendly interface.

Logo
programming language aimed at children and other beginners. The programme is best known for the 'turtle graphics' which are used to draw geometric shapes and patterns.

Modem
a device used to connect a computer to the Internet (via a telephone line).

Mouse
a pointing device — makes interacting with a computer very intuitive.

Peripheral
an extra device connected to a computer, such as a printer, scanner or electronic keyboard.

Software
a program or application which has been designed to allow the computer to carry out a particular task (in effect, a set of instructions).

Spreadsheet
a software application allowing information to be stored in a grid. Particularly useful for storing and manipulating numerical information. Examples include Excel.

Word processor
a software application that is used for working with text, sometimes described as an electronic typewriter but much more useful. Examples include Word and Clarisworks.

Good sources of information:

Glossary of PC Terminology
http://homepages.enterprise.net/jenko/Glossary/G.htm

Free Online Computing Dictionary
http://wombat.doc.ic.ac.uk/foldoc/index.html
PC Webopaedia http://www.pcwebopaedia.com/

Computers and mathematics: staff questionnaire

Please spend 10–15 minutes completing this. Responses will be used to focus our IT INSET.

1. How confident do you feel about using the computer for mathematical activities?

2. Which areas would you like to develop with children?

3. Do you have experience of different types of software: a) personal use or b) with children? (*please give examples of activities*)

	Personal use	Work with children
spreadsheets / databases		
floor robots / Logo		
drawing programs		
mathematical or adventure games		

SECTION 1
Getting started

The activities in this section are important 'curtain raisers' for your INSET programme. On one level they are useful exercises, which provide an opportunity to list and review the resources you have in school, and which highlight the references to IT in the National Curriculum for mathematics. On another level these activities allow you the opportunity to judge the needs of colleagues:

- how familiar they are with the available software

- how aware they are of the explicit National Curriculum references and children's entitlement

- any concerns they may have about using IT

- what skills and knowledge they have that could be drawn upon in future sessions

- how adept they are at recognising opportunities to use IT to enhance work in mathematics

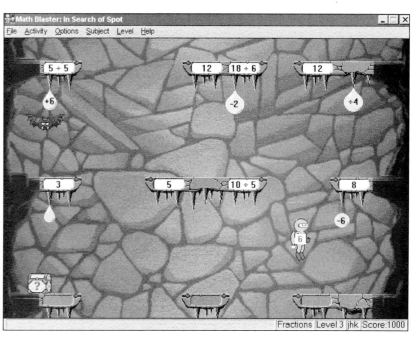

Becoming familiar with the software available in school is an important first step in gaining confidence and expertise in IT.

Timings

Activity 1:
Software audit   1 hour

Activity 2:
Mathematics, IT and the
National Curriculum   40 mins

Activity 3:
Using IT to enhance
mathematics teaching   50 mins

Activity 1
Software audit

You will need

Access to all computers

Copies of Sheet 1A 'Audit of mathematics programs' (one for each pair)

Copies of Sheet 1B 'Large applications and small software' (one for each pair)

Copies of Sheet 1C 'Mathematical things to do on a computer' (one for each pair)

Time

1 hour

If time is short the first part of the activity could be set up in advance of the follow-up discussion.

Purpose

The main purpose of this activity is to involve all the staff in an audit of the mathematics software available in school. You may well have one or more computers dating from the mid-80s that are still capable of running useful software; you may have other top-of-the-range multimedia machines that came bundled with a range of educational software you haven't yet fully explored.

The second part of the activity helps you consider as a staff the range of mathematics that can be done with a computer, and to begin to match these possibilities with the software available in your school.

The activity will engage staff in thinking about the following questions:

- what mathematics software do we have?
- what do we use it for?
- what else could we use it for?
- what do we need in order to use it well?

What to do

Part 1

Explain the purpose of the activity as outlined above.

Organise staff into pairs and agree on which computers each pair will examine. Give each pair a copy of Sheet 1A 'Audit of mathematics programs' to fill in. Allow half an hour for this. If staff are dispersing around the school then be strict about the time to meet up. Spend this time circulating among the groups.

Part 2

Give a copy of Sheet 1B 'Large applications and small software' to each pair. It is interesting to see which category teachers prefer. The larger applications — sometimes called 'content-free' or 'generic' software — take time to learn and require teachers to devise activities for use with them (see Activities 5–9). Smaller software is often more structured and easier to get started with, but usually requires complementary activities away from the computer (see Activity 10).

Ask teachers to put the software from their audit lists into one or other category and check that everyone agrees on the categorisation.

Hand round copies of Sheet 1C 'Mathematical things to do on a computer'. Ask teachers to match these different types of mathematical activities with the potential of the software on their audit sheets. The list of 'mathematical things to do' is not definitive, so tell staff to add to it if they want to. You might want to ask the staff to work in bigger groups at this point.

Collect in all completed sheets. You might want to compile an overview (possibly as a poster to put up in the staffroom) or refer to these again at a later date.

 20 minutes

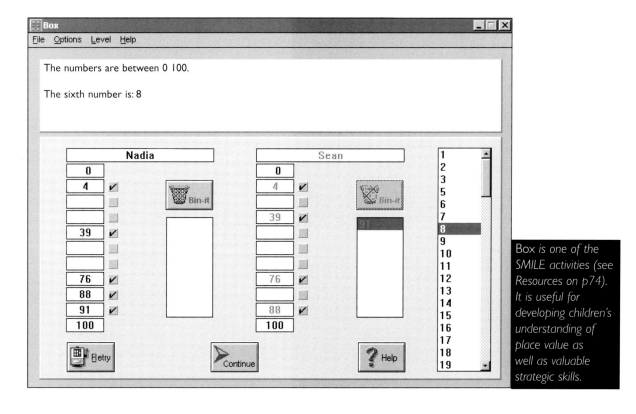

Box is one of the SMILE activities (see Resources on p74). It is useful for developing children's understanding of place value as well as valuable strategic skills.

Some issues that may arise in discussion

- Are the older computers such as the BBCs or Nimbus 186s worth keeping?

- Are some programs too complicated to use with children?

- What's the point of using such-and-such a program?

- Might children think that such-and-such a program is just a game? Does this matter?

- Wouldn't children be better off doing similar work in their books?

Audit of mathematics programs

Room [   ]   Computer [   ]

Which programs does this computer have?

What might the programs be used for?

Large applications and small software

Please list all applications and software in the following categories:

Large applications   These provide general tools which enable a variety of problems to be posed and solved.

Small software   This is designed to be used in particular ways determined by the software author.

Examples
Excel (Spreadsheet)
Information Workshop (Database)
Logo

Examples
Animated Numbers
SMILE mathematics games and activities
Number Shark

Mathematical things to do on a computer

- explore number patterns

- draw shapes

- design a repeating geometrical pattern

- record information

- sort information

- play games

- change the size and shape of objects or print

- practise a multiplication table

- write a short program

- practise number recognition

- create algorithms

- construct graphs

- see 'what would happen if . . .'

- test ideas

Use this box to add some of your own ideas:

-
-
-
-
-

Activity 2

Mathematics, IT and the National Curriculum

Purpose

This activity builds on what teachers learned in Activity 1, aiming to consolidate their understanding of the mathematical potential of the software available in school. The National Curriculum for Mathematics makes no mention of particular software packages, although there are several references to computers, many under the umbrella of 'pupil opportunities'. The implication is that teachers need to decide for themselves what software to use in their schools.

Staff will work together to identify which programs could be linked to which statements from the Programmes of Study for Mathematics. They will also have opportunities to see how the IT and mathematics curricula can be linked, particularly through the use of content-free software such as Logo, databases and spreadsheets.

This activity will help identify:

- which aspects of IT and mathematics are being covered well in school

- which areas would benefit from further development

You will need

Copies of Sheet 2 'Computers in the Mathematics and IT Programmes of Study' (one for each group)

Large sheets of sugar paper, glue, scissors and felt-tipped pens

Time

40 minutes

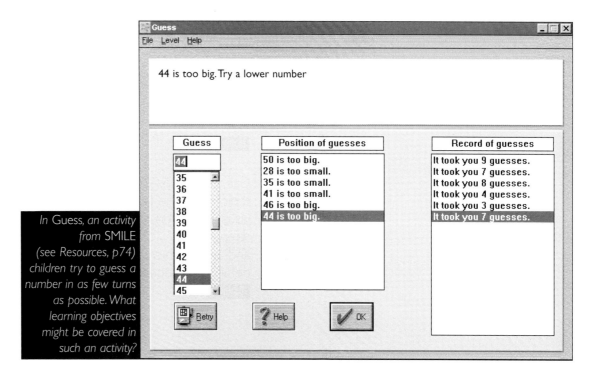

In Guess, an activity from SMILE (see Resources, p74) children try to guess a number in as few turns as possible. What learning objectives might be covered in such an activity?

What to do

Ask the teachers to work in groups of three or four. Give each group a copy of Sheet 2 'Computers in the Mathematics and IT Programmes of Study'. Ask them to cut the sheet up into statements and group together items that might use the same type of software.
`5 minutes`

Each group should then use these statements to create a poster on a large sheet of sugar paper, using the following headings:

NC statement	Which software to use	How well covered

Ask the teachers to stick the National Curriculum statements in the first column, grouped as they agreed in the first part of the activity. In the second column they should list any software which could be used in teaching about this curriculum area. In the third column the teachers should use a code to indicate how well that aspect of the curriculum is covered in their classes. The code suggested is as follows:

☺ Confident that this is being covered well

😐 OK, but would like to do more in this area

☹ This area is not addressed well

This key can be displayed on a flip chart for teachers to refer to.
`25 minutes`

Call the groups together and ask them to share their work. The face symbols should give a clear visual indication of where staff feel their strengths and weaknesses lie. As a staff, discuss, and agree, which software should be covered in detail in subsequent sessions.
`10 minutes`

Handling data is an area of mathematics that can be greatly enhanced by use of appropriate software.

Computers in the Mathematics and IT Programmes of Study

KS1 U&A 4b 'consider the behaviour of a programmable toy'	**KS1 IT 2b** 'enter and store information'
KS1 Number 1f 'use computer software, including a database'	**KS1 IT 2c** 'retrieve, process and display information that has been stored'
KS1 Shape, Space and Measures 1b 'use IT devices'	**KS1 IT 3b** 'give direct signals or commands that produce a variety of outcomes, and describe the effects of their actions'
KS2 Number 1b 'use calculators, computers…as tools for exploring number structure and to enable work with realistic data'	**KS2 IT 2b** 'use IT equipment and software to organise, reorganise and analyse ideas and information'
KS2 Shape, Space and Measures 1c 'use computers to create and transform shapes'	**KS2 IT 3a** 'create, test, modify and store sequences of instructions to control events'
KS2 Handling Data 1c 'use computers as a source of interesting data, and as a tool for representing data'	**KS2 IT 3c** 'explore the effect of changing variables in simulations and similar packages, to ask and answer questions of the "What would happen if…?" type'

Activity 3

Using IT to enhance mathematics teaching

You will need

Copies of Sheet 3 'Topic planner — homes and houses' (one for each pair)

National Curriculum/ Numeracy Framework documents

Sugar paper, pens

Time

50 minutes

Purpose

The previous two activities considered the range of software available in school, and how it can be used to teach the National Curriculum for mathematics and IT. This activity goes a stage further by starting with a popular cross-curricular topic and thinking about ways of enhancing children's mathematical work on that topic through using a computer. The key here is integration — the computer should be used as a general tool or resource to enhance children's mathematical work in cross-curricular contexts.

This activity aims to help teachers:

- understand that they need to teach children the basics of a particular software application in order to use it when an appropriate opportunity arises

- identify useful contexts in which children can use their computer knowledge and skills

- identify which software packages they feel confident about using in their general teaching and which they don't (these can be studied in greater depth in later parts of the INSET programme)

What to do

Ask the staff to work in pairs and look at Sheet 3 'Topic planner — homes and houses'. For each of the suggestions teachers should identify the mathematics that children will be doing, including opportunities for 'Using and Applying Mathematics'.
`15 minutes`

Next ask the pairs to choose one or two of the tasks suggested and to plan them in more detail. They should think about the mathematical knowledge and skills, and IT skills, needed to complete the task.
`10 minutes`

Call the staff together and discuss their work so far.
`5 minutes`

For the next part of this activity it would be useful for staff to work in twos or threes with others who teach children in the same age range. Ask staff to choose a cross-curricular topic and to identify opportunities for using the computer to enhance mathematical work in that area. They should do this as a quick brainstorm, listing their ideas on a piece of paper.
`10 minutes`

Call the groups together and ask them to share their work.
`10 minutes`

Suggested topics

Birds and Flight

Journeys

Celebrations

Our School

Shops and Markets

Toys

Transport

Ourselves

Food

These topics are taken from the 'Starting from Themes' books, published by BEAM, which are designed to provide ideas for mathematical activities in cross-curricular contexts. Alternatively, planning groups might like to look at any topics on which they are going to be working during the year. Where school planning is subject-based, look instead at contexts in History, Geography, Science or Art that could give opportunities for use of mathematical software.

The best computer activities challenge children to think. Many also provide non-judgemental feedback when they go wrong a great asset to learning.

Many programs enable children to produce smarter-looking work, much more quickly, than they could by hand. This allows them to concentrate on the task, and the mathematics, rather than the mechanics of producing neat diagrams.

Topic planner — houses and homes

➡ Use Logo to draw a house twice the size of one given.

Maths links:

➡ Use a drawing or painting program to design a wallpaper pattern.

Maths links:

➡ Use a database to record information about houses and homes near the school.

Maths links:

➡ Use a spreadsheet to compare the cost of different household items from a variety of sources.

Maths links:

➡ Use a drawing program to design the floor layout of a house.

Maths links:

Further suggestions:

SHEET 3

SECTION 2

Exploring software

This section offers some starting points for using different mathematical software, including activities to try out as a staff and with children.

The first activity compares the computer with paper and pencil as a tool for tackling two different mathematical tasks, leading to a discussion on the value of the computer. Further activities in this section focus on particular types of program. In each case you will find some or all of the following:

- a staff handout containing the very basics in terms of commands and vocabulary

- a main activity to try out together

- further activity suggestions

- a sheet which you could make into an overhead projector transparency (OHT) which contains key points for discussion about the application

Where staff are asked to try activities with children you should build time in to the INSET sessions when you can review children's work and discuss any issues that have arisen about particular software.

Choices about which activities to do with children will depend to a large extent on children's previous experience, so no suggestions are given as to age suitablility. One issue that is likely to arise is how to adapt activities for different classes.
And of course teachers will always need to bear in mind the question, 'What mathematical learning is taking place?'

Timings

Activity 4:
What does the computer do?   50 mins

Activity 5:
Databases   1 hour

Activity 6:
Logo   1 hour

Activity 7:
Spreadsheets   1 hour

Activity 8:
Graphics programs   50 mins

Activity 9:
Floor robots   45 mins

Activity 10:
Small software programs   50 mins

Activity 4

What does the computer do?

You will need

Access to computers (one computer for every two or three people)

Software: database/spreadsheet and Logo

Plain paper, 1 cm squared paper, compasses, protractors, rulers, pencils

Copies of Sheet 4A 'Activities' (one for each person)

Copies of Sheet 4B 'IT and children learning mathematics' (one for each pair, or written up large on a sheet of paper, or reproduced as OHT)

Time

50 minutes

Purpose

Many people are unsure about what computers can do. There is the parent with little personal experience who says, 'Computers are not the way I was taught maths', the child who thinks that the computer is doing something magical, and the teacher who, although committed to using computers, is unsure what mathematical skills, knowledge and understanding are involved.

This section focuses discussion on what the computer does by asking staff to do two activities using both a computer and more traditional 'paper and pencil' methods. Each activity has two parts, a set task and a follow-up. It is important that each is completed.

What to do

Split the staff into two groups, give out Sheet 4A 'Activities' and explain the task. You could either get both groups to do both activities, with one group using computers and the other using traditional methods, or have each group stick to one task but do it first using traditional means and then on the computer.

 5 minutes

Set the groups to work. Tell them to list the mathematical skills and ideas they are using as they complete the activities.

 30 minutes

The groups then feed back to each other about the mathematics they have been doing and the processes they used. Round off the discussion by considering the statement on Sheet 4B 'IT and children learning mathematics'. Ask teachers, in pairs, to discuss the following questions:

- Which of these aspects are relevant to the two activities?

- Which match other experiences of teachers using IT with children?

 15 minutes

Some issues that may arise in discussion

- How did you tackle the problem when you were using pencil and paper?

- What was different about doing it on the computer?

- What advantages were there to using the computer for each of these activities?

- How much time do children need to spend on traditional activities?

Activities

Worms

Using Logo

A worm travels 10 mm then turns 90° right;
it then travels 20 mm and turns 90° right;
it then travels 40 mm and turns 90° right.
It repeats this whole operation several times.

Use either squared paper or Logo to recreate the path of the worm.

Now change one of the numbers in the pattern (keep to a multiple of 10).

What do you predict what will happen?

What if you changed the angle?

Journey to school

Using a database or spreadsheet

A survey of the adults working in a school produced the following information about how they travelled to school:

bike: 2   walk: 5   bus: 4   car: 7

Use this information to construct a pie chart using either compasses and protractor or a computer database or spreadsheet program.

One member of staff who previously cycled passes her driving test and now travels to school by car; update your pie chart to show this information.

A new member of staff is appointed, who walks to school; again, update your pie chart to show this information.

IT and children learning mathematics

IT provides five major opportunities for children learning mathematics:

learning from feedback

observing patterns

exploring data

teaching computer skills

developing visual imagery

taken from 'Primary Mathematics with IT' (published by NCET)

Activity 5
Databases

You will need

Access to computers (one computer for every two or three people)

Database software

Copies of Sheet 5A 'Databases — key vocabulary' (one for each person)

Copies of Sheet 5B 'Footwear information' (one for each pair)

Copies of Sheet 5C 'Why use databases?' (one for each pair or reproduced as an OHT)

Time

1 hour

Purpose

Databases form one of the most common groups of 'real world' computer applications. On one level databases are simply electronic cardfile systems. To make this link it is useful to compare the way we look up a book on a local library index, or the way the school secretary keeps personal information about the children, with the way that either of these tasks was undertaken fifteen or so years ago. But databases are more than simply electronic cardfiles. The computer allows records to be sorted and information displayed at great speed, and in a variety of different ways; this can allow the user new insights into the information under scrutiny. Databases are ideal tools when working with the interpretation of data — an important element in the National Curriculum as well as in the National Numeracy Project. This is because, unlike 'real world' computer databases, typical school databases allow for the rapid creation of graphs and charts with which children can experiment.

The aim of this activity is to develop teachers' understanding of the basic vocabulary of database programs. The activity involves working on a task, and sharing and reflecting on experiences of using database programs with children.

What to do

Divide the staff into small groups, each with a computer. Give the groups copies of Sheets 5A, 'Databases — key vocabulary' and 5B 'Footwear information'. (Remember: databases differ in the way they work and you may wish to supplement the vocabulary list with instructions on the software you are using.)

 5 minutes

Ask the teachers to look at Sheet 5B 'Footwear information', and to use this information to create a computer database. The sheet shows information about a group of undergraduate students' footwear. Explain that, because of shortage of time, the actual collecting of data is being skipped. With children, this stage is one of the most crucial and should not be skipped unless for exceptional reasons.

5 minutes

23

Now ask each group to create a blank 'form', set up different 'fields', and complete a 'record' for each student (see the vocabulary sheet on p5 for definitions). Particular things to check for are:

- Does the software allow drop-down lists? (If so, a range of possible responses can be pre-set.)

- How does the software distinguish between numeric and alphabetic fields? (This is important when it comes to drawing certain types of graph.)

- What commands are needed for saving and printing work? (A good practice with creating databases is to save work after each new record has been added.)

`20 minutes`

Once the database has been set up, teachers should explore the different sorting and graphing facilities of the database program.

`20 minutes`

For the final part of the session, structure some general discussion about using databases around the points on Sheet 5C. As a staff, reflect on the different ways that you already use databases with children and agree on some further activities to try out with your classes; make sure you arrange a time to meet and review the children's work

`10 minutes`

Some issues that may arise in discussion

- Should we use ready-made databases, or should children always set them up from scratch?

- What mathematical skills, knowledge and concepts are relevant to database work?

- How might database software be introduced to a class?

- What database vocabulary should we use with children?

- What topics can be usefully tackled with database work?

Suggestions for database work with children

- topics related to current History or Geography work

- children's names, favourite fruit, birthdays or pets

- properties of shapes or numbers

- class book reviews

A sample data collection page from Junior PinPoint (see Resources on p74)

Junior PinPoint - [Form - OURCLASS.PPF]

File   Edit   View   Paper   Arrange   Window   Help

OUR CLASS

1. What is your first name? [   ]   2. When were you born? __ / __ / __

3. Are you a boy or a girl?   ☐ Boy
                               ☐ Girl

4. What colour is your hair?   ☐ Blonde ☐ Black ☐ Brown ☐ Ginger

5. What colour are your eyes?   ☐ Blue ☐ Grey ☐ Green ☐ Hazel ☐ Brown

6. What is you favourite colour?   ☐ Red ☐ Blue ☐ Green ☐ Yellow ☐ Black
                                   ☐ White ☐ Pink ☐ Orange ☐ Purple

7. How tall are you? ___ centimetres

8. How much do ___ kilogrammes   9. What did you weigh when ___ kilogrammes
   you weigh?   you were born?

100%

Databases — key vocabulary

Form
a device for collecting information; an example is given below

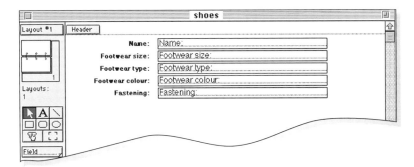

Field
a category of information (the form above has five fields)

Numeric field
a field containing numerical information

Alphabetic field
a field containing written information

Sort
to organise the display of information in a particular way, such as largest to smallest

Search
to look for particular records, such as those with brown footwear

Records
each completed form is a record

Drop-down list
a device that allows a series of multiple choices, such as 'shoes, boots, trainers, others'; drop-down lists are useful because they avoid children mis-typing

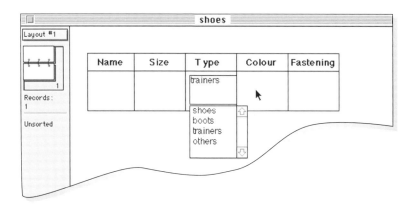

Table view
allows several records to be viewed simultaneously

Common school database software includes Grass, Ourfacts, Clipboard, Information Workshop, Junior PinPoint

Footwear information

NAME	SIZE	TYPE	COLOUR	FASTENING
A	7	Boots	Black	Laces
B	8	Boots	Black	Laces
C	9	Boots	Black	Laces
D	9	Boots	Brown	Laces
E	9	Trainers	White	Laces
F	7	Boots	Blue	Laces
G	6	Shoes	Black	Slip on
H	6	Boots	Yellow	Laces
I	6	Boots	Purple	Laces
J	6	Shoes	Black	Slip on
K	6	Shoes	Black	Laces
L	7	Shoes	Brown	Laces
M	7	Boots	Beige	Laces
N	5	Boots	Black	Laces
O	5	Boots	Black	Slip on
P	5	Shoes	Black	Slip on
Q	3	Boots	Brown	Zip
R	4	Boots	Brown	Buckle
S	5	Trainers	Black	Laces
T	5	Trainers	White	Laces

Why use databases?

- Databases allow opportunities for children to develop classification skills

- Items can be added and deleted over a period of time

- Different groups of children can contribute

- Information collected can be sorted and displayed in different ways

- Databases can be kept for future reference and use

- The software allows children to experiment with different graphs

- As with a 'real world' database, children can experiment with form creation and field definitions

- The use of databases links with the National Curriculum at both KS1 (Number 1f) and KS2 (Handling Data 1c). Representation and interpretation of data is also emphasised in the National Numeracy Project framework

Activity 6

Logo

You will need

Access to computers
(one computer for every two
or three people)

Logo software

Copies of Sheet 6A 'Logo —
key commands' (one for each
person). Before photocopying
this, see 'Which Logo?' on
next page.

Copies of Sheet 6B 'Logo
starter activities' (one for
each computer, or
reproduced as an OHT)

Copies of Sheet 6C 'Why use
Logo?' (one for each person,
or reproduced as an OHT)

Time

1 hour

Purpose

Logo is a programming language that gives
children opportunities to experiment, solve
problems and refine ideas. Turtle graphics are
the most popular aspect of Logo and it is this
aspect that we are concerned with here.
Turtle graphics are particularly good for
children's development of understanding about
shape and space.

Turtle graphics use a number of commands,
such as 'fd 20' or 'rt 75' to move a 'turtle'
around the screen. When using Logo children
ask, 'What would happen if . . .?' questions as a
natural part of the process. Logo 'grows with
the child'; it can be operated at a very simple
level, and each new skill builds on the previous
one, until experienced users can operate at a
very sophisticated level.

It is important that children begin with some
form of Logo at an early age; there will be a
limit to how much a Year 6 teacher can achieve
in one year with a class that has little previous
experience. When developing activities for use
with Logo it is a good idea to prepare a set of
tasks in order of complexity, to ensure a
suitable progression. You would need to include
simple activities that use Logo in direct mode
(as when the turtle is moved in response to
each single command), more complex ones
involving the writing of short procedures (for

example, drawing a polygon using repeats), and
yet more complex ones which use procedures
within procedures (for example, making a
square, then rotating and redrawing it several
times at 30° intervals; or combining several
shapes to make a composite picture). Able Year
5 and 6 children who have used Logo from an
early age will be able to progress to using even
more sophisticated ideas such as variables and
recursion.

These more complex aspects are not covered
in this activity. For teachers working with more
advanced Logo users, there are several good
Logo guides available, and most commercial
educational versions come with reasonable
handbooks. The aim here is to:

● give teachers the opportunity to reinforce
their knowledge and understanding of the
basic vocabulary of Logo

● share and reflect on experiences of using
Logo with children.

For further information, Seymour Papert's
book *Mindstorms*, although originally published
in 1980, remains an excellent introduction
to Logo (see Resources, p74).

What to do

Divide the staff into small groups. You might want to group the teachers so that any beginners are paired with people more experienced in using Logo. Give out copies of Sheets 6A 'Logo — key commands' and 6B 'Logo starter activities'. On one of the computers give a brief demonstration of the main commands. Make sure you point out the command CS (clear screen) so that teachers know they can wipe out any mess they make on the screen.

`5 minutes`

The majority of the session should be spent gaining hands-on experience, as teachers try out some of the suggested activities. Be sure to circulate, picking up on issues that arise for discussion later.

`30 minutes`

Regroup to discuss and reflect on what the staff have been doing. You can use Sheet 6C 'Why use Logo?' to emphasise the value of Logo.

`15 minutes`

Conclude this session by deciding on some Logo activities for staff to try out with children. Arrange a time to meet and review the children's work.

`10 minutes`

Suggestions for Logo work with children

Create a maze on an OHT, attach this to the screen and navigate around the maze

Write your name on the screen

Draw a square, circle, house or flower

Use regular polygons to create a repeating pattern

Recreate a tiling pattern (for example, a Roman mosaic or Islamic pattern)

Some issues that may arise in discussion

- What mathematical skills, knowledge and concepts are relevant to work with Logo?

- How can Logo be introduced to a class?

- How can we help children remember the key commands?

- Do the graphical elements of 1st Logo or WinLogo change the way of working with Logo?

- What are some good basic Logo activities?

- How much structure do we need to provide?

Which Logo?

Logo was originally developed in the late 60s and early 70s and many of the traditional versions (such as that for the RM Nimbus) have a rather dated interface. Contemporary versions of Logo tend to have a more user-friendly graphical interface — for example, Logotron's Winlogo program. You might also want to consider Logo-like programs such as 1st Logo, which reproduce some of the visual aspects in a friendly (though ultimately very limited) way.

Because different Logos use different commands, when using Sheet 6A you will need to check the commands given and add particular information about the version of Logo used by your school, particularly with respect to using the editor, and saving and printing work.

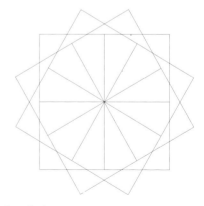

A printout of a piece of work done using Logo. The commands were:
repeat 12 [rt 30 repeat 4 [fd 30 rt 90]]

Logo — key commands

fd 4 move forward 40 steps

bk 40 move back 40 steps

rt 90 turn right 90°

lt 90 turn left 90°

lift/pu lifts the pen from the screen; the pen can now be moved somewhere else without leaving a trace

drop/pd puts the pen back on screen

cs clears screen

ht hides the turtle (useful when printing)

st shows the turtle

program a series of linked commands (for example, repeat 4 [fd 60 rt 90] which will draw a square of size 60 units)

repeat 5 [...] repeats five times whatever is inside the brackets

setpos [x y] (where x and y refer to horizontal and vertical coordinates) will move the turtle to the point with those coordinates

setpos [0 0] returns turtle to centre of the screen

Logo starter activities

- Set up an 'on-screen' obstacle course: use Blutack or pieces of tape stuck to the screen, agree starting and finishing points, then navigate the turtle around the 'obstacles'. Here you are using Logo in 'direct mode'.

- Investigate the use of the repeat command to draw different regular polygons.

  For example, repeat 4 [fd 40 rt 90] will draw a square — but how would you draw a regular triangle, pentagon or hexagon?

  What about a 20- or 30-sided polygon?

- Write a Logo program to recreate either of the following diagrams. What is the most efficient way to do this?

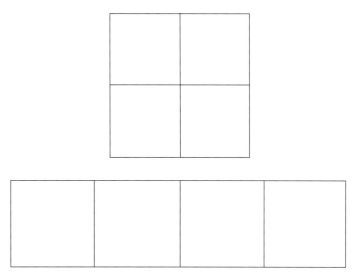

- Use the Logo editor to write, then modify, your program — here Logo is being used in a simple problem-solving exercise.

Why use Logo?

> 'Logo does not teach children mathematics but makes them mathematicians'
> *Seymour Papert (inventor of Logo)*

- Logo is an ideal tool for investigating and solving problems

- Logo motivates by giving instant feedback

- Logo encourages 'thinking about thinking', because procedures can be examined and modified at any time

- A small number of commands can do a lot — and they can be built up in a natural way

- Logo requires children to think and act logically

- Logo allows children to develop and practise estimation of angles and lengths

- The turtle and its movements give a visual representation of mathematical ideas

- Logo immerses children in the language of movement

- Through using Logo children explore shape and space in an active way; the appeal of Logo might be its open-ended nature, but it involves some very specific geometrical learning (for example, 'what is a hexagon?', 'what is 90°?')

SHEET 6C

Activity 7
Spreadsheets

You will need

Access to computers (one computer for every two or three people)

Spreadsheet software

Copies of Sheet 7A 'Spreadsheets — key functions' (one for each person)

Copies of Sheet 7B 'Spreadsheet activities' (one for each pair)

Copies of Sheet 7C 'Why spreadsheets?' (one for each person, or reproduced as an OHT)

Time

1 hour

Purpose

Spreadsheets, like databases, are applications that are used in the real world, although their use is fairly specialised. Spreadsheets are particularly useful for managing and exploring large amounts of essentially numerical information — they certainly look and feel mathematical.

Spreadsheets have a reputation for being difficult to master, and their classroom uses are not immediately apparent. This means they have often been ignored in primary schools. However, modern spreadsheet software such as Excel and Clarisworks are actually quite easy to use (compared to older spreadsheets such as Grasshopper) and, with knowledge of just a dozen or so functions, a lot can be achieved.

This activity aims to explore the potential of spreadsheets. Even if staff decide not to use them with children, experience suggests that understanding the value of spreadsheets can do wonders for the mathematical confidence of adults.

What to do

Divide the staff into small groups. You might want to group the teachers so that beginners are paired with more experienced people. Give out copies of Sheets 7A 'Spreadsheets — key functions' and 7B 'Spreadsheet activities'. On one of the computers give a brief demonstration of the different commands mentioned in the vocabulary sheet.
`10 minutes`

The majority of the session should be spent gaining hands-on experience. Teachers should try out some of the suggested activities and print out the worksheets created. (This is also good practice when children are using spreadsheets as it allows for the examination of results away from the screen. Printouts can also be photocopied and used as the basis of group discussion.) Beginners might benefit from reviewing each of the functions described on Sheet 7A. Be sure to circulate, picking up on issues that arise and noting them down for discussion later.
`30—40 minutes`

Regroup to discuss and reflect on what everyone has been doing. Sheet 7C 'Why spreadsheets?' can be used as an OHT or handout to emphasise the value of spreadsheets.
`15 minutes`

- Could we use ready-made spreadsheets in class or should children always set them up from scratch?

- What mathematical skills, knowledge and concepts are relevant to work with spreadsheets?

- Which children might benefit from using spreadsheets?

- How should we introduce the vocabulary of spreadsheets to children?

- What further activities can children use a spreadsheet for?

Suggestions for spreadsheet work with children

One child sets up a 'function machine' and the other children investigate the output for various different inputs (The 'protected cell' command is useful for setting up a spreadsheet for children to explore; this enables input numbers to be changed without the formula being displayed.)

Explore the relationship between the area and perimeter of a rectangle

Create a magic square — that is, an arrangement of the digits 1 to 9 in which the total of numbers in each row, column and diagonal is the same

Set up a database of class body measurements such as foot length, arm length, head circumference — the ratio of any pair of these can be explored (Be wary when dealing with height and weight, subjects that can cause some children great distress.)

Investigate which of a range of products give the best value for money

Explore various growing patterns

	A	B	C	D	E	F	G
1	Number	Double	Add 4	Multiply by 5	Add 20	Divide by 10	Take away original no.
2	?	=A2*2	=B2+4	=C2*5	=D2+20	=E2/10	=F2–A2
3							

Setting up a spreadsheet for the first 'think of a number' puzzle (see Sheet 7B)

Spreadsheets — key functions

- A **spreadsheet** consists of a grid of **cells**; each **cell** is identified by a grid reference (A1, A2, B1, B2 and so on). The letters refer to the columns, the numbers to rows.

- The space immediately above the letters identifying the columns (A, B, C and so on) is called the **edit bar** or **formula bar**. Click on a cell and its cell reference is shown on the left of the edit bar; the contents of the cell are shown on the right.

EDIT BAR			
A	**B**	**C**	**D**
1			
2			
3			

- Clicking in the top left-hand corner of the grid highlights the whole **spreadsheet**, which is useful for changing its entire format. (Highlight the whole spreadsheet then play around with the 'column height' and 'row height' settings to make the **cells** larger or smaller.)

- Click on a **cell** and information (numbers, dates, prices…) can be written in it. (Press **'enter'** before moving to another cell.)

- A **formula** is a mathematical operation, usually combining the contents of two or more cells in some way or operating on the contents of one cell. (Enter '4' in cell A1, '6' in cell B1 and the **formula** '=A1+B1' in cell C1 to explore this.)

- A **cell reference** is information in one cell which refers to information in another cell. This means that the information in the **cell** containing the reference will change when the **cell** it **refers** to is updated. (In the example above change the value in A1 to '7' and see what happens in cell C1, which **refers** to A1.)

- The **'Fill Down'** command enables information to be copied quickly to other cells. (Highlight cells A1 to C8 and do **'Fill Down'**. Now change the numbers in cells A2 to A8, see what happens in cells C1 to C8.)

- The **keyboard buttons** you will need for working with mathematical formulas are the following:

[+]	add	[−]	subtract
[×]	multiply (above the 8)	[=]	formula
[/]	divide (below the question mark)		

Spreadsheet activities

Think of a number

For these puzzles, set up the spreadsheet so that the operations build up in a sequence across a horizontal row of cells; use **'Fill Down'** to copy the sequence and then experiment by changing the number in column A — several solutions are then visible simultaneously.

Puzzle 1

Think of a number. Double it. Add 4. Multiply by 5. Add 20. Divide by 10. Take away the original number. What is left?

Change the first number. What happens? Why? Does it work with decimals or negative numbers?

Puzzle 2

Think of a number. Multiply by 11. Add 5. Take away the original number. Subtract 5. Divide by 10.

Change the first number. What happens? Why? Does it work with decimals or negative numbers?

Money problems

How can a spreadsheet be used to model these?

Problem 1

If I start with £2 and it doubles every week, how long will it be before I have £1 million?

What if I started with £3, or £5, or £7?

Problem 2

I win £10 million on the lottery; I spend half in the first month, half of what remains in the second month, and so on. How long is it before I'm down to my last £100?

Times tables with a spreadsheet

Recreating something familiar like a multiplication table is a good way to get familiar with spreadsheets. There are several ways of doing this; what follows is just one suggested method.

Highlight cell A1 and type '1' then press **'enter'**

Highlight cell A2 and type '= A1 + 1' then press **'enter'**

Highlight cell A2 and do **'Fill Down'** to A10

Highlight cell B1 and type '2' then press **'enter'**

Highlight cell C1 and type '= A1 * B1' then press **'enter'**

Highlight cell C1 and fill down to C10

Highlight cell B2 and type '= B1' then press **'enter'**

Highlight B2 and fill down to B10. What has happened?

Change the '2' in cell B1 to 3 or any other number. What happens?

Why spreadsheets?

- Spreadsheets are useful where information is frequently repeated

- Spreadsheets enable many calculations to be performed simultaneously

- Unlike most calculators, spreadsheets record all the numbers being used in a calculation

- Spreadsheets facilitate exploration of number patterns and numerical data (see National Curriculum for KS2 Number:1b 'use calculators, computers…as tools for exploring number structure')

- Spreadsheets enable children to focus on problem-solving

- A spreadsheet can be used as a database (and may actually be better than a database when dealing with numerical information)

- A spreadsheet can encourage children to ask (and answer) questions of the type 'What if…'

- A spreadsheet with internal links will automatically update each dependent value if one value has changed, a feature useful in exploring number and number patterns as well as in calculating 'for a purpose'

Activity 8
Graphics programs

You will need

Access to computers (one computer for every two or three people)

Computer drawing software or desk-top publishing (DTP) software; also tessellation or tiling software

Copies of Sheet 8A 'Graphical software activities' (one for each person)

Copies of Sheet 8B 'Graphical software — questions' (one for each person)

Time

50 minutes

Purpose

Most school computers have some sort of graphics program, and newer DTP programs, such as Microsoft Publisher, have similar facilities built in. However, many of these programs are used without any explicit acknowledgement of their mathematical potential. Children can be seen happily drawing shapes, stretching, turning and resizing them, all essentially mathematical transformations, yet they do not make the connection with more traditional 'rotation and reflection' activities.

Children also enjoy working with more obvious shape manipulation software, such as 'My World' screens or VersaTile, and tessellation programs such as Reptile and Tesselmania. It could be argued that this constitutes good preparation for working with the new dynamic geometry software now in use in secondary schools.

The aim of this activity is to:

- give teachers an opportunity to explore available software

- make a clear connection to the mathematics involved

- allow teachers to reflect on the value of using this software with children

What to do

Divide the staff into small groups. Before the staff disperse, give out Sheets 8A 'Graphical software activities' and 8B 'Graphical software — questions' and read through them with the group. The sheets contains some ideas to try out and some questions to reflect on.
 10 minutes

The majority of the session should be spent gaining hands-on experience, exploring some of the software available and trying out some of the suggested activities. Remind the teachers to leave at least 5 to 10 minutes at the end of the session to fill in Sheet 8B. Be sure to circulate, picking up on issues that arise and noting them down for discussion later.
 25 minutes

As a staff, reflect on the different ways that you already use graphics software with children and choose some further activities to try out with your classes. Make sure you arrange a time to meet and review the children's work.
 15 minutes

Graphical software activities

Try out one or more of these activities and print out the results.

1 Draw a rectangle or other shape.

Find out:

- how to rotate it ('turn' it) by different amounts

- how to reflect it ('flip' or 'mirror' it) horizontally/vertically

- how to enlarge or reduce it

- how to distort it ('skew' or 'shear' it)

Try the same with a line of text, a composite shape (two or more shapes joined together) or a clip art image

2 Use the program to build a figure made of recognisable shapes, such as a house, a rocket, a snowman or a castle

3 Use the program to build up a tessellation of hexagons or other shapes

4 Try out any other special effects features of the program (look for words such as 'transformation', 'blend', and 'envelope')

Graphical software — questions

Note down some thoughts in answer to these questions.

- To what extent have you been addressing the National Curriculum requirement in KS2 Shape, Space and Measures 1c to 'use computers to create and transform shapes'?

- What specific aspects of the shape and space program can you cover through using a computer?

- Use this box to make a note of the mathematical language that you have been using.

- Can these computer activities be an adequate substitute for playing with real shapes?

- What would be good activities to ask children to do with this software?

Activity 9
Floor robots

Note — this session is best located in the school hall

You will need

Several floor robots such as Pip or Roamer

Metre sticks and building blocks

Copies of Sheet 9A 'Roamer activities' (one for each person)

Copies of Sheet 9B 'Using floor robots' (one for each person, or reproduced as an OHT)

Time

45 minutes

Purpose

Working with programmable floor robots enables children to develop their spatial sense in a very active way. Given appropriate challenges, this work provides opportunities for the development of a range of problem-solving skills.

Several floor robots are available; Roamer (Valiant Technology) is probably the most common and the activities here refer to it. Pip (Swallow Systems) can also be used for these activities.

It is often said that using floor robots is an essential 'pre-Logo' activity. However, using programmable robots also constitutes valid mathematical activity in its own right. This activity will give staff the opportunity to:

- explore and acknowledge the mathematics implicit in using floor robots

- consider ways of introducing and using floor robots with children.

What to do

Divide the staff into small groups so that there are two or three people to each computer. Before the group disperses, give out Sheet 9A 'Roamer activities' and give a quick demonstration of the basic Roamer commands.

The majority of the session should be spent gaining hands-on experience, exploring the software and trying out some of the suggested activities. Be sure to circulate, picking up on issues that arise and noting them down for discussion later.

Regroup to discuss and reflect on what the staff have been doing. Sheet 9B 'Using floor robots' can be used here, either as an OHT or as a handout, to emphasise the mathematical value of using floor robots. These ideas can also be linked to relevant statements from National Curriculum Programmes of Study.

Conclude this session by asking the staff to choose some Roamer activities to try out with children. Arrange a time to meet and review the children's work.

Some issues that may arise in discussion

- What mathematics are we doing?

- How should we introduce Roamer to the class?

- How can we familiarise children with the commands? Should some be hidden (perhaps covered with sticky tape) to begin with?

- Would it be useful to re-program Roamer to use different units? (See instruction booklet for details.)

- What are some suitable Roamer activities for each class?

Suggestions for robot work with children

Play 'Person Robots': one child is blindfolded; the others give instructions on how she or he should move.

Create an obstacle course for Roamer in the school hall. Use skittles and other PE equipment as obstacles.

Make a large floor map of the streets near the school and move Roamer around it.

Sit in a circle and send Roamer from person to person.

Draw a large spider's web on the floor. Place various insects around it for Roamer, dressed as a spider, to catch.

Make a large number line in Roamer-sized units, toss dice and program Roamer to move up and down the line according to the dice-numbers. (You could try using a dice with halves on it too.)

Working with the Roamer enables children to develop their spatial sense and provides opportunities for the development of a range of problem-solving skills.

Roamer activities

Forward, Back, Right, Left	all need to be followed by a number
CM	Clears the memory; press twice when Roamer is turned on or before a new set of instructions is programmed
W	Wait
R	repeat, use with [ ] brackets

Consult your Roamer/Pip instruction booklet for more details.

- Use metre sticks, large bricks, or other objects to build a rectangular race track for Roamer (3 m by 2 m is an ideal size). Program Roamer to complete a whole circuit.

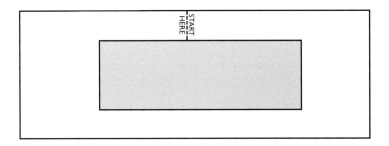

- Create a large floor number line (0–10) on which the distance between numbers is exactly one Roamer length. Now program Roamer to go from 0 to 10, stopping at every even number. (Make use of the repeat function.)

- Draw a large compass on the hall floor and place Roamer somewhere near it, pointing north. Use either an eight-sided spinner or cards marked with the eight compass directions to choose a new direction for Roamer to face. Program Roamer to turn to face the new direction; repeat several times starting from each new position.

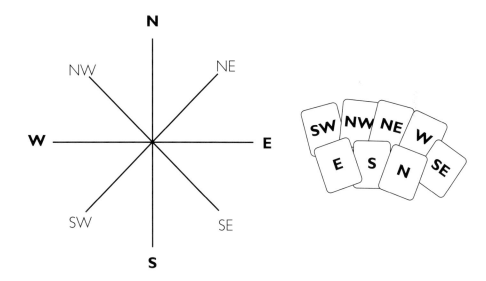

Using floor robots

Work with floor robots addresses National Curriculum KS1 U&A 4b: 'Consider the behaviour of a programmable toy' and is referred to in the National Numeracy Project's Framework Shapes strand for Years 1 to 3.

When using floor robots, children...			
...explore directions — left, right	...explore movements — forwards, backwards	...estimate length and angle	...develop strategies for problem-solving
...develop their spatial sense	...use spatial language	...communicate ideas	...play and work collaboratively

Activity 10

Small software programs

You will need

Access to computers (one computer for every two or three people)

Mathematics software programs such as SLIMWAM or SMILE disks, *Animated Numbers, Hooray for Henrietta, MathsBlaster, Crystal Rain Forest.*

Sugar paper and pens

Copies of Sheet 10A 'Hooray for Henrietta' (one for each person)

Copies of Sheet 10B 'Questions to consider about program…' (two for each group)

Copies of Sheet 10C 'Whole school issues' (one for each person, or reproduced as an OHT)

Time

50 minutes

Purpose

Previous activities have focused on a range of generic applications where the onus is on teachers to set up relevant mathematical problems or investigations with which the software can help. This activity takes a look at a range of smaller, more structured, programs where the software author has designed a mathematical game or set some mathematical questions (often within a game-like format) in such a way that there is a clear educational intention. The difference between types of software has previously been noted (see Activity 1).

Because there is such a range of this type of software no attempt is made to describe many programs in detail or to catalogue them all; however these programs share similar characteristics particularly in the way that there is built-in feedback for the user.

The purpose of this activity is to:

- consider the usefulness of various small programs with respect to the mathematics presented

- discover who might benefit from the programs (this is not always made clear in program documentation)

- find out which software has a facility for a teacher to keep track (on disk) of children's achievements, and how this facility works (useful if you are intending to make extensive use of one particular program)

- explore the extent to which program settings can be modified to meet needs of particular children

- explore the degree to which programs can be used independently

- consider how these programs can complement other mathematical activities using other resources

What to do

Before the session, set up a range of small software (as many different programs as you have). To increase the range you could contact various suppliers (see p74 for addresses) — many will be happy to supply demo disks. Remind staff of the distinctions between different types of software (Activity 1) and ask them to describe the use of any of these programs.

`5 minutes`

Hand out and discuss Sheet 10A 'Hooray for Henrietta'. This sheet describes how one program can be used productively for developing particular aspects of numeracy and offers some hints on the need for caution in using this and similar software.

`10 minutes`

Staff should now, in pairs, explore the software available, and answer the questions on Sheet 10B 'Questions to consider about program…'. Aim for each pair to study at least two different programs.

`20 minutes`

When the group reconvenes ask for quick feedback based around these points, then consider the wider issues raised in Sheet 10C 'Whole school issues'.

`15 minutes`

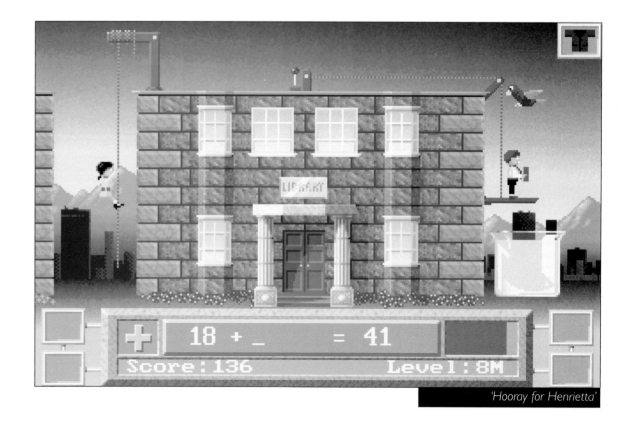

'Hooray for Henrietta'

'Hooray for Henrietta'

This is an example of a basic 'drill and practice' program. Children answer a succession of addition, subtraction, multiplication or division questions. Teacher control includes choosing the operations, setting the difficulty — ranging from single-digit to four-digit sums — and setting the response time. Results of individual children can be monitored. As children answer correctly, Henrietta advances along a path, ultimately rescuing her husband-to-be from a nasty fate.

Which of the following are good/bad/indifferent uses of computer time?

- Children in a Year 3 class are working at mental strategies for addition of two 2-digit numbers. The teacher sets the program for this type of question (presented in a horizontal format) and over a fortnight all of the children in the class have an opportunity to use the program during their numeracy hour. The teacher regularly uses the monitoring facility to find out how children are progressing and to note any questions that they are finding difficult.

- After using the program each child has to complete a sheet giving examples of the questions asked and explaining in their own words what mental methods they have used. Away from the computer during the same period children are working at two 2-digit number addition using 100 grids and empty number lines, and different methods are discussed during whole class plenaries.

- Year 6 children use this program when they have finished their other mathematics work. They choose to work at an unchallenging low level and after a while begin amusing themselves by deliberately getting questions wrong.

- Some able Year 5 children have been introduced to paper and pencil methods for long multiplication. Their teacher sets up Henrietta to produce questions such as 46 × 27. Concerned that they must get to the end of the game, the children secretly use a calculator to find the answers.

- Some Year 2 children are having difficulty with quick recall of their basic subtraction bonds. The teacher sets the program to the appropriate level and operation and over a period of time the group are targeted to spend part of their numeracy hour working at Henrietta with a classroom assistant, who prompts them when stuck. Gradually the teacher reduces the response time, encouraging faster recall of the basic subtraction facts.

Questions to consider about program

- What sort of mathematical learning is involved in this program?

- Who might the program be suitable for, and how adaptable is it?

- Does the context help or hinder the mathematical learning?

- Could an activity be set up away from the computer to complement the on-screen activity?

- To what extent could children use the program independently?

- Are there any other features that you like/dislike about it?

Whole school issues

- What aspects of numeracy can we address through these programs? (Refer to the National Curriculum or Numeracy Framework for details.)

- What are the advantages/disadvantages of these programs (compared to the large generic software packages)?

- How should we organise and monitor the use of these programs?

- How can we ensure children don't regard these programs simply as games?

- Are these programs a good use of computer time?

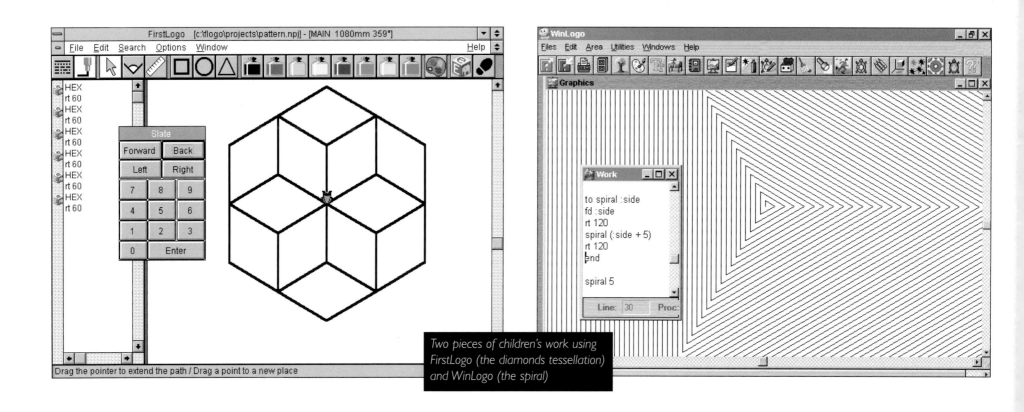

Two pieces of children's work using
FirstLogo (the diamonds tessellation)
and WinLogo (the spiral)

Section 3
Issues in using IT

This section considers many of the key classroom and whole-school issues involved in the use of computers for mathematics — although most of the issues have implications for computer use in general.

How are computers organised? How is their use monitored? What role should a teacher play when children are engaged in computer-based activity? What is the profile of the school's computer work? How are parents involved? These are some of the many questions that arise when discussing the use of computers for mathematics. And each question can have many answers. The activities in this section will help teachers to:

- reflect on some answers to these questions

- develop a shared understanding of these key issues

- work towards a consensus on how to move the school forward in using computers for mathematical activity

It is important that use of the computers is organised fairly and efficiently — and that children know how the system works.

Activity 11

Organising computer use

You will need

Copies of Sheet 11 'Organisational issues' (one for each person)

Large sheets of sugar paper and pens

Time

50 minutes

Purpose

When it comes to practicalities, computers have little in common with other classroom resources. A number line, for example, has no need to be plugged in, is cheap to buy, is easily replaceable and can be used by everyone simultaneously. Computers, as we know to our cost, are very different. The organisational issues that surround computer use can, if not properly acknowledged and dealt with, create disenchantment, particularly where teachers are less than enthusiastic to begin with.

These organisational issues clearly apply to the use of computers in general. However it seems pertinent to consider these as part of a 'computers and mathematics' INSET programme. If teachers are to be adventurous in their use of mathematics software, then removing obstacles to efficient and effective computer use is an essential first step.

The aims of this activity are to enable staff to:

- have a frank and open discussion about issues and concerns surrounding computer usage

- make positive suggestions as to how the whole school might begin to move forward in its use of computers

What to do

Divide the staff into groups of three or four and ask the groups to brainstorm any organisational issues that arise concerning use of computers. They should list these on large sheets of sugar paper.

 10 minutes

Hand round Sheet 11 'Organisational issues'. Ask teachers, in pairs, to choose one or two issues, either from their sheet or from the brainstorm, and to come up with a list of suggested solutions that staff could try out. These could be based on practice that has worked for individuals in the past, or new ideas that people feel would be useful for the whole of the staff to try out. You might want to be selective when using this sheet, focusing teachers on issues of particular concern in your

20 minutes

Call the whole group together and ask teachers to feed back their suggestions. These should be written up on a large sheet of paper. Staff should agree to try out some of the suggestions, and arrange a time to review any changes to practice.

 20 minutes

Organisational issues

- How can computers be integrated into the daily life of the class?

- How can equal access be assured for all children?

- Where is the best place to put the computer?

- How many children should work at the computer at any one time? Should this number always be the same?

- How can the 'keyboard talk' be monitored, ensuring it remains on task?

- Do all children need to have a turn on every program?

- How can we keep track of who has used the computer?

- How can we ensure that children's time is used efficiently?

- How can 35 children be taught to use a new program?

- How can classes make use of each other's computers?

- How can the knowledge and expertise of different adults and children be used throughout the school?

- How can children who get stuck be helped whilst the rest of the class needs teaching?

- How can children be helped to feed back on their computer work to other class members?

- How can other adults (such as teaching assistants, parents, language support teachers) usefully work with children at the computer?

- How can the computer be used to demonstrate ideas to children?

SHEET 11

Activity 12
Equal opportunities

You will need

Copies of school policies for IT and equal opportunities

Copies of Sheet 12A 'Recent research' (one for each person)

One enlarged copy of Sheet 12B 'Equal opportunities and computers' (or reproduced as OHT)

A3 sheets (one for each group) with the following headings:

Equal opportunities and computers	
Issue	What to do

Time

45 minutes

Purpose

Equal opportunities issues are clearly pertinent to computer use in general, but they are particularly worth looking at as part of this INSET program, because both mathematics and IT are curriculum areas where certain children may be at risk of underachievement.

Issues considered in this activity range from the traditional worries about computers be seen as a 'male domain' to the accessibility of software to children from varied ethnic backgrounds and different abilities. A newer concern is that, with the increased popularity of multimedia computers at home, a new technologically under-privileged class is being created, consisting of those children without access to such machines. However, at present the majority of children do not have access to home computers (excluding games consoles).

The aims of this activity are to:

- raise awareness of equal opportunity issues

- enable staff to move forward collectively with respect to addressing equal opportunities

What to do

Distribute Sheet 12A 'Recent research' and ask staff to reflect on it quietly and then spend a few minutes jotting down their reactions.
 5 minutes

Ask the staff to work in groups of three or four and compare their notes. Give out the A3 'Equal opportunities and computers' sheets and ask the groups to draw up a list of equal opportunity issues that are pertinent to their work with children and computers. Ask them also to write down some suggestions as to how these issues can be addressed.
Pin up Sheet 12B 'Equal opportunities and computers' and circulate amongst the groups, suggesting further ideas for discussion from this sheet.
 20 minutes

Allow time for groups to feed back their ideas.
 10 minutes

Conclude by looking at the school's IT and equal opportunities policies. Staff might feel that these need amending in the light of the discussion.
 10 minutes

Recent research

In a recent OFSTED publication by Mike Askew and Dylan Wiliam, *Recent Research in Mathematics Education 5–16*, it says: 'Computers can have a substantial positive impact on pupils' achievement in mathematics'.

However, there is also a caution:

'One major concern over the use of information technology that has not been addressed in any significant way is that access to computers is not equitable. Pupils in economically disadvantaged areas, those from ethnic minorities, and females have less access to computers both at school and at home. Unless these issues of access are resolved, computers, despite their significant potential for remedying inequality, may only serve to reinforce it.'

Reaction

Equal opportunities and computers

- Are staff aware which children have computers at home?

- Is there any difference between boys and girls in their computer knowledge?

- Do girls and boys like using the same software?

- Do all children appear equally confident at using the computer, regardless of ethnic origin?

- Which children are quick to volunteer to solve 'computer problems' such as loading, saving and printing work?

- Do single-sex or mixed pairs work better at the computer?

- Is positive discrimination justified? (For example, should girls or children without home computers have first turns with new software?)

- Does the school promote positive images of a range of adults using computers?

- Do children with special needs need special software? Could you find ways for such children to access the same software as their classmates?

- Is computer use (or lack of it) ever used as a privilege or punishment? Is this justified?

Activity 13

Assessment and record-keeping

Purpose

Having consistent and structured systems for assessing and recording children's IT work is useful for a number of reasons. For class teachers, it provides diagnostic feedback on pupils' developing computer skills, and provides feedback on how successfully different software packages have enhanced children's mathematics work. For the school as a whole it provides a way of ensuring progression in the use of IT and a balanced use of the different software packages.

During this activity staff consider different types of record-keeping and will identify useful formats to try out. It is important that teachers feel a sense of ownership, and that the sample *pro formas* are adapted to suit the school's current needs. It is not envisaged that all six formats would be used by a school.

The aims of this activity are to:

- consider how to assess children's mathematics while they are working on the computer

- consider the issues involved in assessing children's computer work

- agree on the trialling of some types of self-assessment and record-keeping formats

You will need

Copies of the various assessment *pro formas*, Sheets 13A to 13F (one of each for each group)

Copies of Sheet 13G 'Notes on the assessment sheets' (one per group)

Time

30 minutes

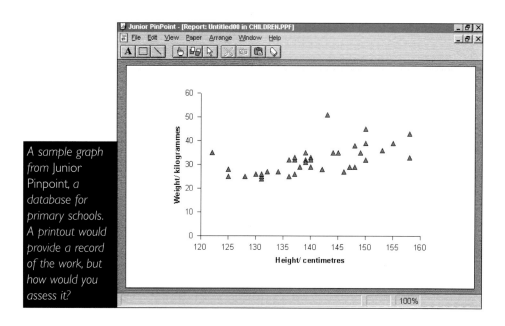

A sample graph from Junior Pinpoint, *a database for primary schools. A printout would provide a record of the work, but how would you assess it?*

What to do

Divide the staff into groups of three or four and ask the groups to talk about any assessment and record-keeping that they do with respect to computers.

They should then look at the various *pro forma* record sheets offered here (Sheets 13A to 13F) and spend some time considering the advantages and disadvantages of each one. Point out that these sheets are intended as suggestions and starting points for discussion, and are not meant to provide ready-made solutions. Ask the groups to focus discussion on ways of adapting one or more of the sheets to suit the school's needs — or writing their own. (Some deal with different levels of assessment and record-keeping so you may prefer to focus on the forms that reflect current concerns.)

15 minutes

Call the whole group together and ask teachers to feed back their suggestions. Make sure some decisions are made on trialling one or more forms (written from scratch or adapted from those provided here). Arrange a time to meet for feedback and a final decision.

10 minutes

Some issues that may arise in discussion

- What is it we are looking for when assessing this kind of work, the IT or the mathematics?

- Should we have separate record-keeping for IT and mathematics? Why?

- What observations might be considered significant?

- Who will the records be useful for?

- How can the assessment help with future planning?

- How will using this record complement other school assessment and record-keeping?

Assessments at KS1 might include basic computer management skills such as turning on the computer and loading work, and simple tasks such as shaping a letter or digit using Logo.

Self-assessment checklist 1

Name [   ]   Date [   ]

I can use the computer to ...	
write my initials using Logo	✓
draw a square using Logo	
make a [ ] using Logo	
play a game called [ ]	
sort information	
draw a graph	
draw some shapes and rotate and reflect them	
use a spreadsheet to do [ ]	
save my work	
load my work	

Self-assessment checklist 2

Name ....   Date ....

Today on the computer I worked with

We used

This is what we did

I learnt that

Next time on the computer I would like to

IT record

Name [   ]   Date [   ]

Program	Date	Activity	Observations

Class record sheet

Class _____

Activity _____

Software package _____

Children	Date	Activity	Observations

Observation Sheet

Observation of [pupil's name]

Worked alone/with	
Activity	
NC refs	
Software used	
Child's approach to the activity	
Child's confidence with the computer	

Did the child…	Yes	No
load the program?	☐	☐
save the work?	☐	☐
print the work?	☐	☐

Printout of work attached   Yes ☐   No ☐

What this sample shows about child's mathematical understanding

Further development

Whole school planning sheet

School record of progression, mathematics and IT

	Reception	Year 1	Year 2	Year 3	Year 4	Year 5	Year 5
Floor robots							
Logo							
Data-handling							
Spreadsheet							
Drawing program							
Small software							
Other							

Notes on the assessment sheets (13A–13F)

13A Self-assessment checklist 1

This should be adapted to reflect the computer work undertaken by the class. Children can read through the list themselves, or it can be used as the basis for a teacher-led discussion with a small group. This type of self-assessment is a good way of developing children's self-confidence and independence.

13B Self-assessment checklist 2

Children can use this individually or in pairs to make a written account of their work, and reflect on recently completed computer work.

13C IT record

A sheet like this could be maintained by the class teacher for each class member. It would form a developing account of each child's progress. Records kept in this way could usefully be passed onto the child's next teacher.

13D Class record sheet

This sheet can be used by a class teacher to keep track of which children have used a particular software package; again, this could usefully be passed onto the next teacher.

13E Observation sheet

Using a sheet like this enables a teacher to make a series of structured observations about a child's work on the computer. If all teachers adopt a common format, information can be readily passed among classes and the sheet could also be used productively by other adults working with the class.

13F Whole school planning sheet

This sheet should be enlarged to A3 size. It enables a school to develop a clear progression of computer-based activities by identifying key tasks for different year groups — for example 'all Year 3s should write their initials using Logo'. It should also help ensure that a range of different software is used throughout the school. Note that not all of the cells need be filled: spreadsheets, for example, might only be introduced in Year 4 or 5.

Activity 14

Raising the profile of IT

You will need

Copies of Sheet 14A 'What type of event?' (one for each person)

Copies of Sheet 14B 'Questions parents might ask' (one for each person)

Copies of Sheets 14C 'Useful ideas' and 14D 'Sample statements for a parents' leaflet' (one of each for each group)

Time

50 minutes

Purpose

The purpose of this activity is to think about ways of communicating the successes of the school's work in IT and mathematics to a wider audience, in particular to parents. This is best done through a hands-on workshop or interactive exhibition, together with an ongoing home/school dialogue. It is important to bear in mind that parents will have very varied experience with computers; some will use them at work and have a good knowledge of particular applications whilst others may be completely technophobic — and there may well be a few computer buffs too. Some parents will have — or will be considering the purchase of — a home computer, and many in this situation might want guidance on software that would be appropriate for their children to use. Other parents may be alarmed about some of the negative publicity computers get — stories about the addictiveness of violent games, health implications and so on.

Working together as a group and planning an exhibition or other event can help cement the staff confidence about using IT — and that is likely to be one of the positive features of your 'computers and mathematics' INSET programme.

It is assumed that you have already agreed to some kind of special 'IT and Mathematics' event; the aim here is to:

- identify and agree on the type of event you wish to set up (since all staff will be involved, it is essential to have a consensus)

- begin to consider what needs to be done

As the event is going to include parents in some way it is also pertinent to consider their possible questions about the way computers are used in the school.

What to do

Staff should work in groups of three or four. Ask everyone to read through Sheet 14A 'What type of event?' (to save time you can circulate this before the staff meeting). Copies of Sheets 14B, 14C and 14D should also be available for teachers to refer to. Each group should draw up a list of reasons for and against holding each type of event in your school.
10 minutes

Ask the groups to share their thoughts and record them on a flipchart — you will return to these later.
5 minutes

Now look at Sheet 14B 'Questions parents might ask'; ask staff to work in pairs considering how they would respond to these questions at a parents' meeting. Questions like these are bound to arise and it is important to have prepared your responses. Be sure to circulate and pick up on issues that arise.
15 minutes

As a whole group, share and discuss possible responses to these questions. It isn't necessary to feed back systematically on every question — just those which seem problematic.
10 minutes

Finally, return to the group's responses to the first activity, written on the flipchart, and try to arrive at a consensus for what type of event you would like to set up. It is important that no-one is left to set it up on their own, so a small group should be nominated to meet with the coordinator and look at the next stage of the planning.
10 minutes

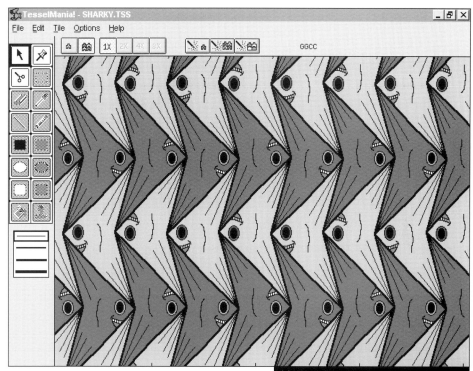

How might you use an activity such as TesselMania in an event for parents?

What type of event?

Consider which of the following events best suits your needs/circumstances:

- A standing exhibition — wall and board displays in a prominent place in the school — including printouts of children's work, word-processed accounts of the computer work they have been doing and some explanation (perhaps by teachers) of the context of the work. This could be made interactive by including one or two computers set up with software for parents to try out.

- An open morning or afternoon when parents are invited to visit classrooms to observe children using computers for a range of mathematical activities.

- A parents' workshop (evening/after school) which would include access to computers with a range of activities. (See Sheet 14C 'Useful ideas' for further detail on this.)

- A special assembly for parents in which children talk about their computer work. Computers can be set up in the hall so that after the assembly children can demonstrate their work.

- A leaflet to inform parents about ways in which the school is using computers to enhance maths activity. This could be used by itself or in conjunction with any of the above. (Sheet 14D has examples of the kind of statements you can include in such a leaflet.)

Questions parents might ask

What is the point of that program? What are they learning?

Why can't they do that without a computer (like I learnt to)?

Aren't they just playing games?

Can he bring in a program that we use at home?

At home all he will do with the computer is play games. How can I get him to use it for something educational?

She uses .... at home; why do you use different computers/ software?

What is the best computer to buy?

What is the best software to buy?

Can I have a copy of that to use at home?

She says that she never gets a turn at the class computer. Is this true?

Useful ideas

Parents' workshop: dos and don'ts

DO

have clear instructions for activities

aim to have at least one adult at each pair of computers plus others 'floating'

have children demonstrating some of the activities

have further displays of children's work

have a separate refreshment area (No drinking coffee around the computers!)

have someone to do a lead talk, such as a local advisory teacher

have a leaflet explaining some of your work

DON'T

worry about using relatively simple activities — most will be new to parents

ask parents to try an activity that you haven't tried yourself first

intimidate parents by using technical jargon

Software circus

Aim to have a full range of the software used in the school; include Roamers, Logo, databases, spreadsheets, drawing programs, mathematics games and structured programs. Parents and children should move around the room/school, trying out the activities available.

Aim to have activities on offer that reflect work done by children throughout the age range. You could use or adapt the suggested computer tasks in Activities 5–10 or any others that you have been using with children.

Remember that your aim should be to show parents how children are using computers to enhance their mathematics, *not* to try to teach parents how to use the programs in any great depth.

The vocabulary and command lists for databases, Logo and spreadsheets (Sheets 5B, 6A and 7A respectively) may be useful additional handouts. Sheets 5C, 6C, 7C and 9B, which consider the rationales for using different software, can be enlarged and displayed in appropriate places.

Who to ask to help

- a business sponsor
- a local computer shop
- IT or mathematics advisors/inspectors
- neighbouring secondary school mathematics/IT department

Sample statements for a parents' leaflet

Over the last few months we have been working as a staff to develop our use of computers with children, with the aim of enhancing their learning of mathematics. This leaflet has been written to inform you about our work in this area.

What teachers use computers for

Like many other adults, teachers use computers in their everyday work. The uses we make of computers include: writing letters home, designing worksheets, recording marks, creating displays and tracking money brought in for the school trips.

How computers enhance the learning of mathematics

IT can provide five major opportunities for learning mathematics:

- learning from feedback
- exploring data
- developing visual imagery
- observing patterns
- 'teaching' the computer

The National Curriculum for Mathematics includes several direct references to using computers.

In school we use computers for many aspects of mathethatics. For example, we use computer databases to collect and sort various kinds of information and to make graphs our results; we use floor robots and Logo to investigate spatial ideas; we use a variety of small software programs to practise our number operations.

Our computer work complements other ways of teaching mathematics and we are committed to ensuring that all children have the opportunity to explore what can be done with computers.

Computer games and mathematics

As we all know, children like to play games, and we do use some learning programs that have a game-like structure which we find really motivates children. Although some of the computer games available in shops are violent or, at best, mindless, there are others that your children would enjoy that do involve a serious amount of problem-solving and mathematical reasoning, such as Lemmings and Tetris. There are also simulations like SimCity and Transport Tycoon which involve modelling (Building cities and managing transport systems, respectively) — these are computer age equivalents of such traditional board game favourites as Scrabble or Monopoly.

How to help your child

- Talk to them about their work: What programs have they been using? What does it do? What have they learnt from using the program?

- Take them to the computer club at your local library; many have programs similar to those we use in school.

- Come into school and see what we are using a computer for (check with your child's teacher for appropriate times).

If you would like more information please contact your class teacher or our IT coordinator.

SHEET 14D

Appendices

Mathematics sites on the internet

Presented here is a short look at World Wide Web sites that can be useful in mathematics education; it concentrates on major sites which tend to be most stable and easy to access. The majority of the sites listed here contain links to several dozen others, and in some cases these links are themselves well annotated. This means that, once connected, a few clicks can lead to a myriad of different items — from reference material and downloadable worksheets through to reviews of textbooks. For the main part, mathematics education materials on the Web consist of useful resources for teachers, rather than interactive sites for children to use. More of the latter are beginning to appear but they often require a fast connection and a powerful computer to make using them worthwhile.

Recent government initiatives in the UK may well see the development of further home-grown resources. Many of the US-based sites have been developing for a number of years and tend to be, at present, better organised. The quality of the ideas and activities, as well as the presentation of them, is variable — on many sites resources are submitted by enthusiastic class teachers rather than professional writers. Particularly when new to using the Intenet, it is easy to get carried away by the sheer range and amount of what is available; we should remember to apply the critical awareness to Web-based resources that we would apply to other educational resources, be they books, tapes or videos.

Ways to use the list of sites

Devote part of a staff meeting to browsing the sites with colleagues, noting useful resources and ideas.

Set up a computer in the staff room with an Internet link for lunchtime use. This will give staff with Internet knowledge the opportunity to show others how to access sites.

Copy the list for staff (and indeed interested parents) to use independently at home or school.

The first page of the BEAM Web site.

Websites to visit

ATM (Association of Teachers of Mathematics)
http://acorn.educ.nottingham.ac.uk//SchEd/pages/atm/
Helpful professional organisation. Includes details of conferences and resources as well as a good set of links to other sites.

BEAM (Be A Mathematician)
http://www.beam.co.uk
Includes details of INSET courses and downloadable extracts from publications, as well as links to other interesting mathematics sites.

Curriculum IT Support for Mathematics
http://vtc.ngfl.gov.uk/resource/cits/maths/
Part of the developing Virtual Teaching Centre, this site is likely to undergo great expansion in the next couple of years.

Dictionary of Measures, Units and Conversions
http://www.ex.ac.uk/cimt/dictunit/dictunit.htm
Exactly what it says — easy to use, would be a good resource for older juniors researching measures.

Egyptian Mathematics
http://eyelid.ukonline.co.uk/ancient/numbers.htm
A good resource — could be used productively by children during work on this topic.

Funbrain Math Baseball
http://www.funbrain.com/math/index.html
Interactive site for children providing basic number practice in a game-like format.

Logo Foundation
http://el.www.media.mit.edu/groups/logo-foundation/
Useful activities, mathematical background, downloadable trial software versions.

Maths Central
http://MathCentral.uregina.ca/

Maths Forum
http://forum.swarthmore.edu/
Two excellent US-based resource sites with dozens of annotated links.

Maths Net
http://www.paston.co.uk/users/mathsnet/contents.html
Good set of resources and ideas for using IT to enhance mathematics activities.

Maths Problem Solving Task Centre
http://www.srl.rmit.edu.au/mav/PSTC/index.html
Australian-based site which focuses on mathematical problem-solving; includes a good selection of open-ended investigations.

Megamaths
http://www.c3.lanl.gov/mega-math/welcome.html
Enables interactive exploration of several mathematics topics.

NRICH
http://nrich.maths.org.uk/
Online maths club with professional backing and sponsorship, for use by pupils as well as teachers.

TIMSS (Third International Maths and Science Study)
http://www.ed.gov/NCES/timss/
Read the results of this major international research firsthand.

Shell Centre for Mathematics Education
http://acorn.educ.nottingham.ac.uk/ShellCent/
Top UK research centre, includes details of work and publications and an excellent set of further links.

UK Schools: Maths Resources
http://www.liv.ac.uk/~evansjon/maths/menu.html
A good starting point for Web browsing for mathematics resources of all sorts.

WWW Virtual Library: Mathematics
http://euclid.math.fsu.edu/Science/math.html
Good for researching pure mathematics topics as well as mathematics education materials.

Resources

Enriching Primary Mathematics with IT

Janet Ainley
Hodder and Stoughton
ISBN 03 40644 02 8

A review of different applications with many excellent ideas for integrating IT with various different topics.

Recent Research in Mathematics Education, 5–16

Mike Askew and Dylan Wiliam
HMSO
ISBN 01 13500 49 1

Comprehensive round up of topical research — very useful starting points for staff discussion.

Mindstorms

Seymour Papert
Basic Books
ISBN 04 65046 74 6

Very readable account of using computers with children, by the inventor of Logo. Despite being nearly 20 years old, this book still has contemporary relevance.

Children Using Computers

Anita Straker
Simon and Schuster
ISBN 18 98255 12 1

Full of classroom examples of use of computers, this book really encourages the use of a whole range of applications.

BECTA (British Educational Communications and Technology Agency) [formerly NCET]

Milburn Hill Road, Science Park, Coventry CV4 7JJ
tel: 01203 416994
http://www.ncet.org.uk/

Comprehensive publications list including software; very useful web site.

Black Cat Software

The Barn, Cwm Camlais, Brecon, Powys, LD3 8TD
tel: 01874 636835
http://www.blackcatsoftware.com

Software includes Information Workshop, First Workshop, Counter and Clipboard.

Inclusive Technology

Saddleworth Business Centre, Delph, Oldham OL3 5DF
tel: 01457 819799

General educational software supplier specialising in catering for children with special needs.

Longman Logotron

124 Cambridge Science Park, Milton Road, Cambridge CB4 4ZS
tel: 01223 425558
http://www.logo.com

Software includes WinLogo, FirstLogo, VersaTile and Junior PinPoint.

REM (Rickett Educational Media)

Great Western House, Langport, Somerset TA10 9YU
tel: 01458 253646

A really comprehensive educational software yearbook including teacher reviews. Very helpful and knowledgeable staff will help track down software from over 250 publishers. Recommended!

Research Machines

New Mill House, 183 Milton Park, Abingdon, Oxford OX2 0BW
tel: 01235 826000

Reliable supplier of computer/educational software packages.

Sherston Software

Angel House, Sherston, Malmesbury, Wiltshire, SN16 0LH
tel: 01666 8404333

Software includes Animated Numbers and The Crystal Rain Forest.

SMILE

Isaac Newton Centre, 108a Lancaster Road, London W11 1QS
tel: 0171 221 8966
http://www.rmplc.co.uk/orgs/smile/index.html

Have been developing innovative secondary maths materials for many years. The classic MicroSmile games programs have recently been rewritten for Windows — excellent for KS2.

Swallow Systems

134 Cock Lane, High Wycombe, Bucks HP13 7EA
tel: 01494 813471

Produce the Pip and Pixie floor robots.

Topologika Software

Islington Wharf, Penryn, Cornwall TR10 8AT
tel: 01326 377771

Software includes Maths Book, Screen Turtle and Numberpics.

Valiant Technology

Valiant House, 3 Grange Mills, Weir Road, London SW12 0NE
tel: 0181 673 2233

Produce the Roamer floor robot and a whole range of support materials.

White Space Software

41 Mall Road, London W6 9DG
tel: 0181 748 5927

Software includes Number Shark.

Acknowledgements

Aimee Buck, Gill Westbrook and Bishop Winnington Ingram CE School, Middlesex

Barbara Carr and Cranford House School, Oxon

Hasan Chawdhry and Globe Primary School, London

Muriel Chester and the Southwark BEAM Group

Anne Clark and St Chad's Primary School, Leeds

Emel Ibrahim and Burnt Ash Primary School, Bromley

Olive Millington and Guilden Morden Primary School, Hertfordshire

Claire Neuberger and Menorah Primary School, London

Yvonne Norman and Honeywell Junior School, London

M O'Grady and Northbourne Park School, Kent

Karen Pearse and Winsor Primary School, London

Jane Prothero and Grimes Dyke Primary School, Leeds

Anne Stone and Squirrels Heath Junior School, Essex

Andrew Warren and Amherst Primary School, Guernsey

Deirdre Wright and St Josephs RC Primary School, Bromley